This Journal Belongs To

Year-At-A-Glance

Seasonal Garden Chore List

Year _____

■ Spring

- [ ]
- [ ]
- [ ]
- [ ]
- [ ]
- [ ]
- [ ]
- [ ]
- [ ]

■ Summer

- [ ]
- [ ]
- [ ]
- [ ]
- [ ]
- [ ]
- [ ]
- [ ]
- [ ]

■ Winter

- [ ]
- [ ]
- [ ]
- [ ]
- [ ]
- [ ]
- [ ]
- [ ]
- [ ]

■ Fall

- [ ]
- [ ]
- [ ]
- [ ]
- [ ]
- [ ]
- [ ]
- [ ]
- [ ]

Monthly Planting Planner

Plant Name	January	February	March	April	May	June	July	August	September	October	November	December

Monthly Garden Chore List

Month _____

- [ ] _____
- [ ] _____
- [ ] _____
- [ ] _____
- [ ] _____
- [ ] _____
- [ ] _____
- [ ] _____
- [ ] _____
- [ ] _____
- [ ] _____
- [ ] _____
- [ ] _____
- [ ] _____
- [ ] _____
- [ ] _____
- [ ] _____
- [ ] _____
- [ ] _____
- [ ] _____
- [ ] _____
- [ ] _____

Monthly Garden Chore List

Month _____

- [ ] _____
- [ ] _____
- [ ] _____
- [ ] _____
- [ ] _____
- [ ] _____
- [ ] _____
- [ ] _____
- [ ] _____
- [ ] _____
- [ ] _____
- [ ] _____
- [ ] _____
- [ ] _____
- [ ] _____
- [ ] _____
- [ ] _____
- [ ] _____
- [ ] _____
- [ ] _____
- [ ] _____
- [ ] _____

Garden-Planning

Garden Plan

Date _____

Use this simple template to plan your garden.
Use each square to represent any size you designate—
2 feet, for example—depending on the size of your garden.
Label plants A,B,C, etc., and fill in the key below.

A _____ x _____   H _____ x _____   O _____ x _____
B _____ x _____   I _____ x _____   P _____ x _____
C _____ x _____   J _____ x _____   Q _____ x _____
D _____ x _____   K _____ x _____   R _____ x _____
E _____ x _____   L _____ x _____   S _____ x _____
F _____ x _____   M _____ x _____
G _____ x _____   N _____ x _____

Square Foot Garden Plan

Date _____

Use this simple template to plan a 4' x 4' square foot garden. Use multiple sheets as necessary. List or sketch plants per square foot.

12"

12"

Gardening Expenses

Item	Quantity	Price	Where Purchased	Date of Purchase	Notes

Gardening Expenses

Item	Quantity	Price	Where Purchased	Date of Purchase	Notes

Fertilizer/Soil Amendment Record

Date	Problem / Deficiency (Soil Test Results / pH levels)	Plant/Area Amended	Amendment/Fertilizer Applied	Notes

Seed Starting Tracker

Plant Name	Seed Source	Date Planted	Germination Date	Transplant Date	Notes (Success rate, germination temp/light, etc.)

Plant Tracker

Plant	Where Purchased	Date Planted	Expected Harvest Date	Date of First Harvest	Date of Last Harvest	Notes

Pests & Problems

Plant	Problem	Course of Treatment	Date(s)	Effective? (Yes/No)	Notes

Plant Profile

Plant _____

Description

Date Planted _____

Exposure _____

Mature Size _____

Days to Harvest / Bloom _____

Care Instructions

Known Problems

How to Harvest

Uses / Notes

Plant Photo / Sketch	Date

Plant Profile

Plant _____

Description

Date Planted _____

Exposure _____

Mature Size _____

Days to Harvest / Bloom _____

Care Instructions

Known Problems

How to Harvest

Uses / Notes

Plant Photo / Sketch

Date

Plant Profile

Plant _____

Description

Date Planted _____

Exposure _____

Mature Size _____

Days to Harvest / Bloom _____

Care Instructions

Known Problems

How to Harvest

Uses / Notes

Plant Photo / Sketch	Date

Plant Profile

Plant _____

Description

Date Planted _____

Exposure _____

Mature Size _____

Days to Harvest / Bloom _____

Care Instructions

Known Problems

How to Harvest

Uses / Notes

Plant Photo / Sketch	Date

Plant Profile

Plant _____

Description

Date Planted _____

Exposure _____

Mature Size _____

Days to Harvest / Bloom _____

Care Instructions

Known Problems

How to Harvest

Uses / Notes

Plant Photo / Sketch

Date

Plant Profile

Plant _____

Description

Date Planted _____

Exposure _____

Mature Size _____

Days to Harvest / Bloom _____

Care Instructions

Known Problems

How to Harvest

Uses / Notes

Plant Photo / Sketch

Date

Plant Profile

Plant _____

Description

Date Planted _____

Exposure _____

Mature Size _____

Days to Harvest / Bloom _____

Care Instructions

Known Problems

How to Harvest

Uses / Notes

Plant Photo / Sketch	Date

Plant Profile

Plant _____

Description

Date Planted _____

Exposure _____

Mature Size _____

Days to Harvest / Bloom _____

Care Instructions

Known Problems

How to Harvest

Uses / Notes

Plant Photo / Sketch

Date

Plant Profile

Plant _____

Description

Date Planted _____

Exposure _____

Mature Size _____

Days to Harvest / Bloom _____

Care Instructions

Known Problems

How to Harvest

Uses / Notes

Plant Photo / Sketch	Date

Plant Profile

Plant _____

Description

Date Planted _____

Exposure _____

Mature Size _____

Days to Harvest / Bloom _____

Care Instructions

Known Problems

How to Harvest

Uses / Notes

Plant Photo / Sketch	Date

Harvest Tracker

Plant _____

Date Harvested	Qty. / Weight	Notes
Season Total:		

Seed Harvesting Tracker

Plant _____

Seed source _____

Date of seed harvest _____

Weight of seeds _____

Seed Harvesting

Selection and collection method	Insect/disease damage

Seed cleaning method and drying time	Storage conditions

Seed Testing

Date sown	Days to germination	Number of seeds sown	Number germinated	Success rate (%)	Notes

Seed Usage

Date	Yield (Qty.)	Qty. Planted	Date Planted	Reserve

Follow this record with the *Seed Starting Tracker* to track the vigor/size of your seedlings, and the *Plant Profile* to track the crop/yield, any problems, etc.

Garden Journal

Garden Journal

Garden Journal

Garden Journal

Garden Journal

Date _____

Garden Journal

Date _____

Garden Journal

Garden Journal

Date _____

Garden Journal

Date _____

Garden Journal

Garden Journal

Date _____

Garden Journal

Date _____

Garden-Planning

Garden Plan

Date _____

Use this simple template to plan your garden.
Use each square to represent any size you designate—
2 feet, for example—depending on the size of your garden.
Label plants A,B,C, etc., and fill in the key below.

A _____ x _____   H _____ x _____   O _____ x _____

B _____ x _____   I _____ x _____   P _____ x _____

C _____ x _____   J _____ x _____   Q _____ x _____

D _____ x _____   K _____ x _____   R _____ x _____

E _____ x _____   L _____ x _____   S _____ x _____

F _____ x _____   M _____ x _____

G _____ x _____   N _____ x _____

Square Foot Garden Plan

Use this simple template to plan a 4' x 4' square foot garden. Use multiple sheets as necessary. List or sketch plants per square foot.

12"

12"

Gardening Expenses

Item	Quantity	Price	Where Purchased	Date of Purchase	Notes

Gardening Expenses

Item	Quantity	Price	Where Purchased	Date of Purchase	Notes

Fertilizer/Soil Amendment Record

Date	Problem / Deficiency (Soil Test Results / pH levels)	Plant/Area Amended	Amendment/Fertilizer Applied	Notes

Seed Starting Tracker

Plant Name	Seed Source	Date Planted	Germination Date	Transplant Date	Notes (Success rate, germination temp/light, etc.)

Plant Tracker

Plant	Where Purchased	Date Planted	Expected Harvest Date	Date of First Harvest	Date of Last Harvest	Notes

Pests & Problems

Plant	Problem	Course of Treatment	Date(s)	Effective? (Yes/No)	Notes

Plant Profile

Plant _____

Description

Date Planted _____

Exposure _____

Mature Size _____

Days to Harvest / Bloom _____

Care Instructions

Known Problems

How to Harvest

Uses / Notes

Plant Photo / Sketch	Date

Plant Profile

Plant _____

Description

Date Planted _____

Exposure _____

Mature Size _____

Days to Harvest / Bloom _____

Care Instructions

Known Problems

How to Harvest

Uses / Notes

Plant Photo / Sketch	Date

Plant Profile

Plant _____

Description

Date Planted _____

Exposure _____

Mature Size _____

Days to Harvest / Bloom _____

Care Instructions

Known Problems

How to Harvest

Uses / Notes

Plant Photo / Sketch

Date

Plant Profile

Plant _____

Description

Date Planted _____

Exposure _____

Mature Size _____

Days to Harvest / Bloom _____

Care Instructions

Known Problems

How to Harvest

Uses / Notes

Plant Photo / Sketch	Date

Plant Profile

Plant _____

Description

Date Planted _____

Exposure _____

Mature Size _____

Days to Harvest / Bloom _____

Care Instructions

Known Problems

How to Harvest

Uses / Notes

Plant Photo / Sketch	Date

Plant Profile

Plant _____

Description

Date Planted _____

Exposure _____

Mature Size _____

Days to Harvest / Bloom _____

Care Instructions

Known Problems

How to Harvest

Uses / Notes

Plant Photo / Sketch	Date

Plant Profile

Plant _____

Description

Date Planted _____

Exposure _____

Mature Size _____

Days to Harvest / Bloom _____

Care Instructions

Known Problems

How to Harvest

Uses / Notes

Plant Photo / Sketch	Date

Plant Profile

Plant _____

Description

Date Planted _____

Exposure _____

Mature Size _____

Days to Harvest / Bloom _____

Care Instructions

Known Problems

How to Harvest

Uses / Notes

Plant Photo / Sketch

| Date |

Plant Profile

Plant _____

Description

Date Planted _____

Exposure _____

Mature Size _____

Days to Harvest / Bloom _____

Care Instructions

Known Problems

How to Harvest

Uses / Notes

Plant Photo / Sketch	Date

Plant Profile

Plant _____

Description

Date Planted _____

Exposure _____

Mature Size _____

Days to Harvest / Bloom _____

Care Instructions

Known Problems

How to Harvest

Uses / Notes

Plant Photo / Sketch	Date

Harvest Tracker

Plant _____

Date Harvested	Qty. / Weight	Notes
Season Total:		

Seed Harvesting Tracker

Plant _____

Seed source _____

Date of seed harvest _____

Weight of seeds _____

Seed Harvesting

Selection and collection method	Insect/disease damage

Seed cleaning method and drying time	Storage conditions

Seed Testing

Date sown	Days to germination	Number of seeds sown	Number germinated	Success rate (%)	Notes

Seed Usage

Date	Yield (Qty.)	Qty. Planted	Date Planted	Reserve

Follow this record with the *Seed Starting Tracker* to track the vigor/size of your seedlings, and the *Plant Profile* to track the crop/ yield, any problems, etc.

Garden Journal

Garden Journal

Date _____

Garden Journal

Garden Journal

Date _____

Garden Journal

Garden Journal

Garden Journal

Date _____

Garden Journal

Date _____

Garden Journal

Date _____

Garden Journal

Date _____

Garden Journal

Date _____

Garden Journal

Garden-Planning

Garden Plan

Date _____

Use this simple template to plan your garden.
Use each square to represent any size you designate—
2 feet, for example—depending on the size of your garden.
Label plants A,B,C, etc., and fill in the key below.

A _____ x _____   H _____ x _____   O _____ x _____

B _____ x _____   I _____ x _____   P _____ x _____

C _____ x _____   J _____ x _____   Q _____ x _____

D _____ x _____   K _____ x _____   R _____ x _____

E _____ x _____   L _____ x _____   S _____ x _____

F _____ x _____   M _____ x _____

G _____ x _____   N _____ x _____

Square Foot Garden Plan

Date _____

Use this simple template to plan a 4' x 4' square foot garden. Use multiple sheets as necessary. List or sketch plants per square foot.

12"

12"

Gardening Expenses

Item	Quantity	Price	Where Purchased	Date of Purchase	Notes

Gardening Expenses

Item	Quantity	Price	Where Purchased	Date of Purchase	Notes

Fertilizer/Soil Amendment Record

Date	Problem / Deficiency (Soil Test Results / pH levels)	Plant/Area Amended	Amendment/Fertilizer Applied	Notes

Seed Starting Tracker

Plant Name	Seed Source	Date Planted	Germination Date	Transplant Date	Notes (Success rate, germination temp/light, etc.)

Plant Tracker

Plant	Where Purchased	Date Planted	Expected Harvest Date	Date of First Harvest	Date of Last Harvest	Notes

Pests & Problems

Plant	Problem	Course of Treatment	Date(s)	Effective? (Yes/No)	Notes

Plant Profile

Plant _____

Description

Date Planted _____

Exposure _____

Mature Size _____

Days to Harvest / Bloom _____

Care Instructions

Known Problems

How to Harvest

Uses / Notes

Plant Photo / Sketch | Date

Plant Profile

Plant _____

Description

Date Planted _____

Exposure _____

Mature Size _____

Days to Harvest / Bloom _____

Care Instructions

Known Problems

How to Harvest

Uses / Notes

Plant Photo / Sketch

Date

Plant Profile

Plant _____

Description

Date Planted _____

Exposure _____

Mature Size _____

Days to Harvest / Bloom _____

Care Instructions

Known Problems

How to Harvest

Uses / Notes

Plant Photo / Sketch

Date

Plant Profile

Plant _____

Description

Date Planted _____

Exposure _____

Mature Size _____

Days to Harvest / Bloom _____

Care Instructions

Known Problems

How to Harvest

Uses / Notes

Plant Photo / Sketch

Date

Plant Profile

Plant _____

Description

Date Planted _____

Exposure _____

Mature Size _____

Days to Harvest / Bloom _____

Care Instructions

Known Problems

How to Harvest

Uses / Notes

Plant Photo / Sketch

| | Date |

Plant Profile

Plant _____

Description

Date Planted _____

Exposure _____

Mature Size _____

Days to Harvest / Bloom _____

Care Instructions

Known Problems

How to Harvest

Uses / Notes

Plant Photo / Sketch

Date

Plant Profile

Plant _____

Description

Date Planted _____

Exposure _____

Mature Size _____

Days to Harvest / Bloom _____

Care Instructions

Known Problems

How to Harvest

Uses / Notes

Plant Photo / Sketch	Date

Plant Profile

Plant _____

Description

Date Planted _____

Exposure _____

Mature Size _____

Days to Harvest / Bloom _____

Care Instructions

Known Problems

How to Harvest

Uses / Notes

Plant Photo / Sketch | Date

Plant Profile

Plant _____

Description

Date Planted _____

Exposure _____

Mature Size _____

Days to Harvest / Bloom _____

Care Instructions

Known Problems

How to Harvest

Uses / Notes

Plant Photo / Sketch	Date

Plant Profile

Plant _____

Description

Date Planted _____

Exposure _____

Mature Size _____

Days to Harvest / Bloom _____

Care Instructions

Known Problems

How to Harvest

Uses / Notes

Plant Photo / Sketch	Date

Harvest Tracker

Plant _____

Date Harvested	Qty. / Weight	Notes
Season Total:		

Seed Harvesting Tracker

Plant _____

Seed source _____

Date of seed harvest _____

Weight of seeds _____

Seed Harvesting

Selection and collection method	Insect/disease damage

Seed cleaning method and drying time	Storage conditions

Seed Testing

Date sown	Days to germination	Number of seeds sown	Number germinated	Success rate (%)	Notes

Seed Usage

Date	Yield (Qty.)	Qty. Planted	Date Planted	Reserve

Follow this record with the *Seed Starting Tracker* to track the vigor/size of your seedlings, and the *Plant Profile* to track the crop/yield, any problems, etc.

Garden Journal

Date _____

Garden Journal

Garden Journal

Garden Journal

Date _____

Garden Journal

Garden Journal

Date _____

Garden Journal

Garden Journal

Date _____

Garden Journal

Garden Journal

Garden Journal

Date _____

Garden Journal

Date _____

Garden-Planning

Garden Plan

Date _____

Use this simple template to plan your garden.
Use each square to represent any size you designate—
2 feet, for example—depending on the size of your garden.
Label plants A,B,C, etc., and fill in the key below.

A _____ x _____   H _____ x _____   O _____ x _____
B _____ x _____   I _____ x _____   P _____ x _____
C _____ x _____   J _____ x _____   Q _____ x _____
D _____ x _____   K _____ x _____   R _____ x _____
E _____ x _____   L _____ x _____   S _____ x _____
F _____ x _____   M _____ x _____
G _____ x _____   N _____ x _____

Square Foot Garden Plan

Date _____

Use this simple template to plan a 4' x 4' square foot garden. Use multiple sheets as necessary. List or sketch plants per square foot.

12"

12"

Gardening Expenses

Item	Quantity	Price	Where Purchased	Date of Purchase	Notes

Gardening Expenses

Item	Quantity	Price	Where Purchased	Date of Purchase	Notes

Fertilizer/Soil Amendment Record

Date	Problem / Deficiency (Soil Test Results / pH levels)	Plant/Area Amended	Amendment/Fertilizer Applied	Notes

Seed Starting Tracker

Plant Name	Seed Source	Date Planted	Germination Date	Transplant Date	Notes (Success rate, germination temp/light, etc.)

Plant Tracker

Plant	Where Purchased	Date Planted	Expected Harvest Date	Date of First Harvest	Date of Last Harvest	Notes

Pests & Problems

Plant	Problem	Course of Treatment	Date(s)	Effective? (Yes/No)	Notes

Plant Profile

Plant _____

Description

Date Planted _____

Exposure _____

Mature Size _____

Days to Harvest / Bloom _____

Care Instructions

Known Problems

How to Harvest

Uses / Notes

Plant Photo / Sketch

Date

Plant Profile

Plant _____

Description

Date Planted _____

Exposure _____

Mature Size _____

Days to Harvest / Bloom _____

Care Instructions

Known Problems

How to Harvest

Uses / Notes

Plant Photo / Sketch	Date

Plant Profile

Plant _____

Description

Date Planted _____

Exposure _____

Mature Size _____

Days to Harvest / Bloom _____

Care Instructions

Known Problems

How to Harvest

Uses / Notes

Plant Photo / Sketch	Date

Plant Profile

Plant _____

Description

Date Planted _____

Exposure _____

Mature Size _____

Days to Harvest / Bloom _____

Care Instructions

Known Problems

How to Harvest

Uses / Notes

Plant Photo / Sketch	Date

Plant Profile

Plant _____

Description

Date Planted _____

Exposure _____

Mature Size _____

Days to Harvest / Bloom _____

Care Instructions

Known Problems

How to Harvest

Uses / Notes

Plant Photo / Sketch	Date

Plant Profile

Plant _____

Description

Date Planted _____

Exposure _____

Mature Size _____

Days to Harvest / Bloom _____

Care Instructions

Known Problems

How to Harvest

Uses / Notes

Plant Photo / Sketch	Date

Plant Profile

Plant _____

Description

Date Planted _____

Exposure _____

Mature Size _____

Days to Harvest / Bloom _____

Care Instructions

Known Problems

How to Harvest

Uses / Notes

Plant Photo / Sketch	Date

Plant Profile

Plant _____

Description

Date Planted _____

Exposure _____

Mature Size _____

Days to Harvest / Bloom _____

Care Instructions

Known Problems

How to Harvest

Uses / Notes

Plant Photo / Sketch | **Date**

Plant Profile

Plant _____

Description

Date Planted _____

Exposure _____

Mature Size _____

Days to Harvest / Bloom _____

Care Instructions

Known Problems

How to Harvest

Uses / Notes

Plant Photo / Sketch	Date

Plant Profile

Plant _____

Description

Date Planted _____

Exposure _____

Mature Size _____

Days to Harvest / Bloom _____

Care Instructions

Known Problems

How to Harvest

Uses / Notes

Plant Photo / Sketch	Date

Harvest Tracker

Plant _____

Date Harvested	Qty. / Weight	Notes
Season Total:		

Seed Harvesting Tracker

Plant _____

Seed source _____

Date of seed harvest _____

Weight of seeds _____

Seed Harvesting

Selection and collection method	Insect/disease damage

Seed cleaning method and drying time	Storage conditions

Seed Testing

Date sown	Days to germination	Number of seeds sown	Number germinated	Success rate (%)	Notes

Seed Usage

Date	Yield (Qty.)	Qty. Planted	Date Planted	Reserve

Follow this record with the *Seed Starting Tracker* to track the vigor/size of your seedlings, and the *Plant Profile* to track the crop/yield, any problems, etc.

Garden Journal

Garden Journal

Garden Journal

Garden Journal

Date _____

Garden Journal

Date _____

Garden Journal

Date _____

Garden Journal

Garden Journal

Date _____

Garden Journal

Date _____

Garden Journal

Date _____

Garden Journal

Garden Journal

Date _____

Garden-Planning

Garden Plan

Use this simple template to plan your garden.
Use each square to represent any size you designate—
2 feet, for example—depending on the size of your garden.
Label plants A,B,C, etc., and fill in the key below.

A _____ x _____	H _____ x _____	O _____ x _____
B _____ x _____	I _____ x _____	P _____ x _____
C _____ x _____	J _____ x _____	Q _____ x _____
D _____ x _____	K _____ x _____	R _____ x _____
E _____ x _____	L _____ x _____	S _____ x _____
F _____ x _____	M _____ x _____	
G _____ x _____	N _____ x _____	

Square Foot Garden Plan

Date _____

Use this simple template to plan a 4' x 4' square foot garden. Use multiple sheets as necessary. List or sketch plants per square foot.

12"

12"

Gardening Expenses

Item	Quantity	Price	Where Purchased	Date of Purchase	Notes

Gardening Expenses

Item	Quantity	Price	Where Purchased	Date of Purchase	Notes

Fertilizer/Soil Amendment Record

Date	Problem / Deficiency (Soil Test Results / pH levels)	Plant/Area Amended	Amendment/Fertilizer Applied	Notes

Seed Starting Tracker

Plant Name	Seed Source	Date Planted	Germination Date	Transplant Date	Notes (Success rate, germination temp/light, etc.)

Plant Tracker

Plant	Where Purchased	Date Planted	Expected Harvest Date	Date of First Harvest	Date of Last Harvest	Notes

Pests & Problems

Plant	Problem	Course of Treatment	Date(s)	Effective? (Yes/No)	Notes

Plant Profile

Plant _____

Description

Date Planted _____

Exposure _____

Mature Size _____

Days to Harvest / Bloom _____

Care Instructions

Known Problems

How to Harvest

Uses / Notes

Plant Photo / Sketch | Date

Plant Profile

Plant _____

Description

Date Planted _____

Exposure _____

Mature Size _____

Days to Harvest / Bloom _____

Care Instructions

Known Problems

How to Harvest

Uses / Notes

Plant Photo / Sketch	Date

Plant Profile

Plant _____

Description

Date Planted _____

Exposure _____

Mature Size _____

Days to Harvest / Bloom _____

Care Instructions

Known Problems

How to Harvest

Uses / Notes

Plant Photo / Sketch | **Date**

Plant Profile

Plant _____

Description

| |
| |

Date Planted _____

Exposure _____

Mature Size _____

Days to Harvest / Bloom _____

Care Instructions

Known Problems

How to Harvest

Uses / Notes

Plant Photo / Sketch

Date

Plant Profile

Plant _____

Description

Date Planted _____

Exposure _____

Mature Size _____

Days to Harvest / Bloom _____

Care Instructions

Known Problems

How to Harvest

Uses / Notes

Plant Photo / Sketch

| Date |

Plant Profile

Plant _____

Description

Date Planted _____

Exposure _____

Mature Size _____

Days to Harvest / Bloom _____

Care Instructions

Known Problems

How to Harvest

Uses / Notes

Plant Photo / Sketch	Date

Plant Profile

Plant _____

Description

Date Planted _____

Exposure _____

Mature Size _____

Days to Harvest / Bloom _____

Care Instructions

Known Problems

How to Harvest

Uses / Notes

Plant Photo / Sketch	Date

Plant Profile

Plant _____

Description

Date Planted _____

Exposure _____

Mature Size _____

Days to Harvest / Bloom _____

Care Instructions

Known Problems

How to Harvest

Uses / Notes

Plant Photo / Sketch	Date

Plant Profile

Plant _____

Description

Date Planted _____

Exposure _____

Mature Size _____

Days to Harvest / Bloom _____

Care Instructions

Known Problems

How to Harvest

Uses / Notes

Plant Photo / Sketch	Date

Plant Profile

Plant _____

Description

Date Planted _____

Exposure _____

Mature Size _____

Days to Harvest / Bloom _____

Care Instructions

Known Problems

How to Harvest

Uses / Notes

Plant Photo / Sketch	Date

Harvest Tracker

Plant _____

Date Harvested	Qty. / Weight	Notes
Season Total:		

Seed Harvesting Tracker

Plant _____

Seed source _____

Date of seed harvest _____

Weight of seeds _____

Seed Harvesting

Selection and collection method	Insect/disease damage

Seed cleaning method and drying time	Storage conditions

Seed Testing

Date sown	Days to germination	Number of seeds sown	Number germinated	Success rate (%)	Notes

Seed Usage

Date	Yield (Qty.)	Qty. Planted	Date Planted	Reserve

Follow this record with the *Seed Starting Tracker* to track the vigor/size of your seedlings, and the *Plant Profile* to track the crop/ yield, any problems, etc.

Garden Journal

Garden Journal

Garden Journal

Date _____

Garden Journal

Garden Journal

Date _____

Garden Journal

Garden Journal

Date _____

Garden Journal

Date _____

Garden Journal

Date _____

Garden Journal

Date _____

Garden Journal

Date _____

Garden Journal

Date _____

Made in the USA
Lexington, KY
30 July 2017